# THE COLOR OF DUSK

ROBIN CATON

OMNIDAWN

RICHMOND, CALIFORNIA

2001

*This book is dedicated to Curt and Laura. Without their love and support, these poems could not have been written.*

ACKNOWLEDGEMENTS
I am grateful to the editors of the following journals for publishing poems from *The Color of Dusk*, sometimes in slightly different versions and/or with different titles:

*five fingers review*: "S Tone"
*Poetry Flash*: "Elegies: Eleven"
*Columbia Poetry Review*: "Matter of Time, 6"
*6ix*: "Breakfast at the Franklin Hotel"; "this"
*Generator*: "In the Museum"; "Black Point Series, #3"; "Prelude to Silence"; "Galapagos"; "East Bay Vivarium"
*syllogism*: "Eight Ways of the Yong Character"; "Matter of Time, 10"
*Fourteen Hills*: "Study for *The Color of Dusk, #3*"; "Study for *The Color of Dusk, #9*"
*BOOMERANG!*: "Preceding Series (Duncan)"
*ROOMS*: "Gray"; "Blue"; "Matter of Time, 3"

Book cover and interior design by Philip Krayna Design, Berkeley, California.

Cover paintings by Justin Hunter.

O MNIDAWN™

Published by Omnidawn Publishing, Richmond, California
www.omnidawn.com · (800) 792-4957

ISBN: 1-890650-08-0 (paper)          9 8 7 6 5 4 3 2 1

♲ Printed in the United States on recycled paper.

# CONTENTS

GRAY

signs of torque

small hairs
grown

    monstrous

here in the entryway
of glass

the book invades

bird resists

the fear of flight
intensifies
                    when

birthing itself from x

and nearness? the way
it darts
syntax of emergency
so that darkness
slips inside

seeds of continents
        wax

what flattens    echoes

*I am in the third*
*Circle, a realm of cold and heavy rain*

*I*   like a housefly
persists

collapse time
elaborate
the passion

if there's age-
lessness
try to imagine
the *ness*

and if it's god
you're listening for?

    wedged forward
    letters spread like cloud
    grammar inarticulable
    except by pause —

PURPLE

# EAST BAY VIVARIUM

Reptilian stillness. The way there
barred by little gate-keepers —
wide-eyed innocents. Bloodless.
*I am    I am*

and underneath, multiple cells
like toilets flushing continuously
rhythmically, formulaically.
Pure structure: *The tangerine*

*bandstand unzips to reveal the pearly*
*sky and all the tired windpipes heave*
*their mixed diaphanous blue pills*
*to a chugging engine in the thick storm.*

The floating I not as angle/line/
angle but as curve/curve/curve
so that all falls back on itself like
eggs in dough.

Fortunate. Fortune.it. The in/
flux in/flight. In/
ternal meanings unleashed. Ins
flying in darkness unable

to land and the flux
waiting like a lover on a mountain
for the hopeless ins,
the magnificent ins.

To be surrounded by silence
and wish the morning into light.
Isn't it something to be appeased by?
This fracturing.

# THE DUCHESS PRAYS

There are three beginnings, the Duchess says. These correspond to the Father, the Son and the Holy Ghost. Although I have made this up, it makes sense.

The first is called "Morning."

I am sitting on a train. We are in France. It starts to rain. Father enters; he is not my father. I give him a name. The hills in the distance are faintly green. Six people leave. The train stops. The watch on my wrist rises through the air like a dream.

The Duchess smiles. The second beginning is called "Night," she says.

We are in France. I am sleeping on a train. Six people enter. I give them a name. Father leaves; he is faintly blue. The watch on my wrist is not my watch. I take a pill. It starts to rain.

The train lurches. Coffee spills from a blue cup. The Duchess strokes a small white dog that sits on her lap and says, the third beginning is my favorite. This one's called "All the Way through Hell."

The train lurches. My coffee spills. I try to drink from a blue cup but it turns green. The watch on my wrist is faintly white. I give it a name. We are in France. Father enters; he rises through the air like a dream.

There are three beginnings, one middle, and one end, the Duchess says. These correspond to the five Books of Moses. Although I have made this up, it makes sense.

The train lurches. Her coffee spills. The hills in the distance are not her hills. There are three beginnings, but only one end, the Duchess says. This corresponds to the one God.

The train stops. The rain starts. She takes a pill and feels faintly green. *Shmai Yisrael Adonai Elohenu, Adonai Echod*, her father says. *Hear, O Israel, the Lord is our God, the Lord is One.*

And although he has made this up, it makes sense.

# BOUNDARY

remarkablemorningtheyareallhere
thepiecesofmyselfIcarryinaslingthe
sestonestheyareknockingagainstm
etheyareturningmythighpurpleand
bluethecolorsofbirdsandIwonderif
mylegwillsimplyflyleavingmeachin
gcrane-likeclutchingthesestonestom
ysideit'suselesstoflingthemfromeac
honeI'dtossanotherwouldemergest
onebornofstoneachild'scairnnobette
rtoleavethemwheretheyarefindtheo
neIlikethebestagrayflatonethree-sid
edwithacrackIfeeltheoptionsinitsspa
cetheparadoxofsplityetsolidsurfaceIh
aveplansforthesestonesI'mgoingtoput
themtouseremarkablemorningIentert
hegardenit'shereIthinkI'llbuildthewall

# MATTER OF TIME, 6

White arrow of the field-drawn sky
I left dreaming behind in favor of angle

Linkages are made in the desert
Twin desires, girded in salt

Numbers, love us!
Each sells something for her bliss

My moments enter backwards
Tell us the story of leaving

Some little tyrant from the dead city
I measure my body by this

# GALAPAGOS

domed bodies    sentient field    sky
a gray that cracks to purple

oh heavenly father    in thee we place
our selves    these selves longing to return
turn again    drawn to starred surfaces

tell us the words for the dissolving mysteries
name the names of those we know and make
them love us    say I am    say robin
shout robin

language winched    illusions of singularity
mockingbird as that two-legged winged
thing    and it, too, satisfied    it, too,
naming in its sweet-throated way the ones
on the beach as    alien

# STUDY FOR *THE COLOR OF DUSK*

*Evening. Bus stop. A talking bird.*
Interviewed, she holds her own

and weeps like Jesus
"privileging the absent salutation."

Father, thou ought to save us
(or something of the sort).

And when, on his talented wings,
the misogynist falters:

*lapsus.*
If the green is green and the white

white, the rest un-burns.
Not that the fabric is empty.

Certainly not!
But the purple flower milking light

from seed? Corporeal self?
*Two children on a train at night,*

*the landscape fading.*
Pardon the flooding, she says.

Bend of the body's birth.
*This is his pain. This is mine.*

Is there? he asks, stroking her
hair. To which she replies,

not often.

GREEN

## PRECEDING SERIES (DUNCAN)

*Often I am permitted*    unwingd O    *to re-turn*

groping    often, often    a certain shaped thing

seeking its longitude    and the permission?

light falling on said meadow    arms out-stretchd

as if from no thing    rising    oft oft often

is the per mitting    is the I of ten    to excavate

this *eadow*    to un-leaf    headless, heedless

the obscene green    so much in the rhythm

of these sounds precedes us    came into the world

came forth    a *meadow*    often, often    obligd

permitted    re-turnd    re-tumbld    arms out-

stretchd    oblique, obscure    I ecstatic    take

O and walk her through a dark center to this the light
[desiring

# WHAT MISHAP

in the air perceives me?
sound arising on the cuff of wind
*nicht wahr?*

old and yellow as fossil
we of the lonely archways
we of the

> *no friend; part us*
> *the ear's no place for death*

holy one, blessed be she, heavy with rock
I am not without
but crowded through these veins

*Wehrnacht*
verge of heaven, mouldering

## ELEGIES: ELEVEN

What you could write, in German, in the 1920's is not what can be written, in English, today. Is not. Is not. Is not. That you could speak with angels and feel them present when you did, this is the miracle. Today the void is well known. No grungy angel with dirty wings looking at you cross-eyed, but a black hole that sucks away at its own edge. The diner and its meal.

To converse with angels is its own delight.

### Conversation With an Angel

Poet: What is the source of our infinite pain?
Angel:

Conversation with angels is never quite right.

There are other considerations. Take philosophy, for example. The influx, twisting, turbulent thought, trying for vision. Four curious wings. The repeat of the vision is necessary. To start and re-start in fits and starts. Working toward angels.

The blackness lifts. There is the outline of a shadow's shadow. Your face freezes, tongue thick as sand, oceans running through you. You want to deliver the final word — curse, or pray, or fall to your knees awestruck. But the

vision plays itself in dull, unsyncopated time and simply:
waits. There are no words. There is no fevered praise.
You are two beasts in a zoo, neither sure who is in the
cage. Will you see more of it? You doubt you can move
as quickly as it likes. You doubt you are the one it has
come for. The transformation continues at a slow pace.
Skepticism re-shapes itself. No words contain this.
You are making progress in your dumb side-show way,
but you feel the angel hesitate. Speaking, touching, all
the human means are too small. You wonder at your lack
of terror. At how ordinary it is.

# MATTER OF TIME, 3

Matter revolutionizes method in the quick regard of sense. The explosive wherewithal fragrant in its particulars. I, caught, retreats in a modicum of sound. Mellifluousness of the weather. We can't escape. See this line? These telephones are fake. Scars create the phony sense of talking. And then. So. Whenever. Patterned language holes. The ontology of this is confusing. We in our own echoed pajamas when suddenly death.... There's a thought! Check the date. If nothing comes of nothing, then time, the angel, flutters in. Do we need code books? My wings are dry. On some back stair, the mind is whistling. On this page angels. On that, the habit of multiplying.

earththroat

a wind

     (moving)

the streets
are falling

once    the bells
twice   the bells

      I am not able

beginning

     *sorrow of light*
     *the color*
     *of grass*

# STUDY FOR *THE COLOR OF DUSK*

light: as the shadow's mask
sleeping inside the gesture of satiety
moments of longing in mirrors
the archways filled with walls
draped, the blue escaped you
markers unfolding a lost life in openness
sense, sense the drums
there were lines in the body like salt
like stone sieved
nothing in that light contained you

# THE DUCHESS SPEAKS OF SPRING

*We must do away with all explanation
and description alone must take its place.*
—L. WITTGENSTEIN

On the last day before the last, I took a train to Paris,
the Duchess says. It was such a lark! A lark? Oh, some kind
of bird. Gray, I think, or black; it hardly matters. You see,
I was on the train when.... Why, the thing is just a bird for
heaven's sake!

Well, well; you needn't take offense. Blue then. No,
green. Green, I suppose.

On the last day before the last, in Paris, the Duchess
says, larks rose over the city like grapes — green grapes.
It was dawn. The sky was pink. From the Place de la
Concorde came a hideous cry and thousands of larks rose
together, wheeled three times around the Eiffel Tower and
plunged into the Seine.

The Seine? Muddy and brown. But the point is —

You're kidding! All right, then: red. A *red* point.

On the last day before the last, I took a train to Paris,
the Duchess says. The sky was pink; the larks were green;
the river, brown. It was such a bloody bore!

RED

11. Open cell with mortar
of direct flower: here is the
garden's source. Apple of
dream in the doctor's eye.
A lust. These are notions
that win her an open stain.          *I am an idolater*
A forest of sky red & green.
Kinsman with an abstract
aim, she forces night. Blue
herons. A culling of verbs.
Neither the will nor stories.

12. The fig's in different
moods again and cries
lost. An absolute text.        *What is it to be God's elect?*
The knife retracts. She
finds herself in hollows.

13. Here is the place from
whence cometh the vision,
all red in the center. A place
of deepness and fastness.
Open unto this my flower,
my small child, my darling.          *No, not one shall be forgotten*
Make fruit of me. The Duchess          *who was great in the world*
winks. A dog barks. I hear
the sea. Corrupt or human?
I am unwell. The pain is green.
And why so merry? My breath
is in branches; I haven't heard.

14. The elements disburse
themselves with play.
These are words and
these an empty bed. All    *Then came the fullness of time*
told, there's something
new to hope for. A crow
with pastries. A hole in-
side a tube inside a jar.

15. Pinks of sky at dawn.
A fledgling bird. No one
feels this wind. Here's
desire's analog: a floating
limb. Each hour a bit of
animal dissolves. Her bed
turns blue. The crow grins.
Fifteen frogs release from
sixteen princes. Cinderella's
slippers start to sing.

*For what significance had it
when Isaac was to be sacrificed?*

16. Coptic ventures: for-
tune's knave among the
piled-up dead. Governance
has left the scene a wonder.
Too much trot. No room        *How the body is perfect*
to make amends. Foreign
children roam the city's slopes.
Look lightly. Stay in jail!
A starry wind blows past.

ORANGE

# BLACK POINT SERIES, #3

So far, the dialectic — the marginalized scratching.
Each week we approach millenium, escalating territories
rove. And here, in the carrot sky, the jangling! *My* hopes,
*my* dreams. These self-reproaches. I would prefer engendering
(the pouring in of gender). Rims. Displacements. In this
sense, innocence. *Not in the music is the music made* abutting
towers, monasteries, the flight of birds. Successful
counterweights to time.

————————

Desire creeps by. The flies are landing. This is
enticement: sand, flies, stench. The massed dead matter
of the ocean.

*folded, dangerous, marbled white*

I would ride these waves.

I would be them.

# THIS

haunch of tree
lip of wave
see this. rising
several intimacies     tongue on tongue
soldering rhythm to breath
more pull     more thrust
wings deliver the final cascade
willing as snow

this head moves like this
tries faith     fades
dismembers

these barriers erect themselves in this
the flooding
conjuring acts
this description dying

and the mote     so embraced
the joinder
the male submersion
see this about me     repeated

easier now to imagine stages
so-called horizons
equal in weight to this
something lifting     becoming glass
the entrance through river exhausting itself

cloistered in the melon air
the metrics of pain
see the mind opening out of itself like this
several envelopes of grieving

# STUDY FOR *THE COLOR OF DUSK*

*I am ill*
followed by

*a place for drowning*
his naked back

functioning now like bread
now like bridges

which best to ignore?
I sense the poignancy in this

the odd bit of information
*dearest love,*

*I left the correctional facility*
*a new gal*

lust is a song
*have been idle for days*

*and now this swollen head*
it doesn't parse

one needs a red of singular dimension
the aptitude for orange

I cry jewels

don't look

the sun's about to spoil

# BREAKFAST AT THE FRANKLIN HOTEL

Solidity escapes in the morning — black taxis, brick facades. London's heaviness.

Woman enters 47. Red cars occupy their space.

There are long pauses. Emptiness of field.

*Anniversary of the Battle of the Somme / Twenty Thousand Killed in Half an Hour*

Perhaps the settled sky relapses, narrowing out like bodies from shells, extending its rubberized center in quadrants. The heart, back to the edges each time, longing for comfort.

What's lost is the condition that permits repeating.

Trying to trick ourselves to stay in *things*. That rose. Reflective paleness of orange turned pink. Shape exacting itself from mass, so that, touched, there's some emblem.

And yet, the quantity of emptiness —

There's heat at the edge. Stars enter us and scatter.

Woman enters 47. Red cars occupy their space.

Listen.

A moth whispers. The steady hum of oscillation.

# WRITING MIND

in here's the wailing    in here's the small
article pinging against itself    the metallic
*o*    wishing and not making itself
concrete    the allowable hollow steel
weathered and unwashed    wiping the
feet of trochees in the bath    water
like toothpicks darting    mixing in the
heated loam    splayed fingers of beggar
girls    even these open hands    words
molding themselves around objects to
display them    edges crawling toward
each other    sharp-lined    the blues
tangential    chimeras of light    sensing
the non-sensible    they sail like origami
boats    impermanence embedded in the

                                    structure

# MATTER OF TIME, 7

viable hour of mastery

these feathers rousing
weight
from lost locations

marry this to me

*my* list    *my* nomenclature

your page
adorned with kisses

# PRECEDING SERIES (STEVENS)

*We say God and the imagination are one* we say
and so saying said and made and did we say
we are we say say we are say say said we say
and God and the imagination we say say one
and one says say God and we say say God and
the imagination and say we say say we are God
some saying is better saying some saying says
something saying some saying says God and
the imagination are one saying God one saying
the imagination one saying some saying is
saying some say some saying is saying something
one says some saying says something God
God says saying is some thing said some said
something God one imagination say one we say
say someone God say some one one God we say
say someone say someone say someone God
some saying is some thing said some saying isn't

WHITE

eternal evening coalesces

the residue opens
confusing
                        prime and
force

we kneel toward and

then cut

I've time

        would not get sound
        before the ancient Hoon

I
that stem instructions
contain outside
is

as the white
at vector is
light-potential

lit    I'm empty

what hour gives what
to is?

I heard no state
out of we

or with
or as

she photographs light
makes it un–
noticed
like little pre–
symbolic tribes

of if
of be

the if
poured more sparks

their call     a food

the I is ended

here          the mineral

collapsing in campfire

mountain-minded space
under flower

the when
is mystery

presences revealing silhouette
where when
may ground

the unconscious
suddenly reaches
the end of human desire

in-negligent magic
then

        a projection

water    water    bodies

music out of
primary heat

amaryllis waltz
that's in &
out

it too
there

attending

combinatory camera
of time
pours containment

she was I

Josiah among much

    motionless
    blue

and for this
each son now
comes to her
as desire

as rags
which have there
an I

day's light comes
for the possible

there's truth
setting
on the mirror

power in a squat mouth

so by the tissue
of many lamps
the substratum
                wanders

only shadows glare
like that wavering
king's city

physical    spelled

arriving like glass
wherever speaking
didn't

BLUE

*There's no such thing as good painting about nothing.*
                    —A. GOTTLIEB and M. ROTHKO

as in this venture
articulate    space
wraps the introspective
moment in blue there's
no such thing as
there's no    such
thing as    thing as
good about    there's
no such good about
thing
as thing as good there's
no    such good
thing
good    good
g    o    o    d    a    s

*good*

as good thing/about
as good thing/as
as good thing/thing
as good thing/no


*thing*

as thing such no there's
as thing such no
there's as thing such
no there's as thing
such no there's as
thing such no there's
as thing such no there's

*thing such*

    no there's as thing such

*such no*

    there's as thing such no

*as thing?*

    such no there's as thing

*good*

```
e   v   e   n   b   l   u   e   e   x   p   a   n   d
s   /   /   /   /   /   /   /   /   /   /   /   e
v   e   n   b   l   u   e   e   x   p   a   n   d   s
e   v   e   n   b   l   u   e   e   x   p   a   n   d
s   /   /   /   /   /   /   /   /   /   /   /   e
v   e   n   b   l   u   e   e   x   p   a   n   d   s
e   v   e   n   b   l   u   e   e   x   p   a   n   d
s   /   /   /   /   /   /   /   /   /   /   /   e
v   e   n   b   l   u   e   e   x   p   a   n   d   s
```

so that I know    so that I can tell a good thing
so that I know    so that I can tell an empty thing
a no thing    so that I can stay on the side of good
and not slip unaware    unconscious into no from
good    into empty from full so that I
so that I

I

I

*thing*       *thing*

*thing*       *thing*

          *thing*

BLACK

# S TONE

Is there a purpose for the misshapen form of things —
stone like a bear, a hedgehog, a dehydrated mouse
(furless, soundless, cheeseless mouse)?


*To all desire for escape you must oppose contemplation and its resources.*
—F. PONGE

Observation of a stone over several days:
So far pressed into itself it hums with the vibrance
of enjambment.


Impossible to want if you're a stone.

Sentence: *The stone wanted a bath.* Truth value: negative.
What audacity: to deny a stone desire!


Cutting. Sitting on. Entering. The air around.
Rained on. Thrown. Singular and plural. The
implications of past tense. Identity of. How we
are all becoming.

"Stone!"

Call it.

Its non-responsiveness. The inability to embody
in a word that self-identifies. Stone as: forever alien to
itself.

So much breath without a nose!

Proliferation of unmarked doors, progress barred. DO
NOT NOT ENTER HERE.

Rotten monk! Unforgiving trickster!

The soul: larger or smaller than one stone?

One without others: dysfunctional, lonely, misplaced.

*No stone is an island.*

# EIGHT WAYS OF THE YONG CHARACTER

First stroke: the dot.


eye of the fourth wren to the left in the willow that hasn't wept
motion of moon in windowless temple on top of a bleak hill
philosophical answer to identity crisis of peripatetic child
mind approaching the extinction of story through light
day that a mother leaves and a father, joyful, sings
mark of return of the concept, *this is not a pipe*
living incarnation of the wish-fulfilling gem
product of dream times the reality of hell
not the master who murdered the king
structural guide to the theory of red
crows clustered on a broken field
umbra of grass echoing birth
silence of the small gods
time it takes to sneeze
night of invisible sun
willingness to listen
six bees waiting
spare change
fold of book
daybreath
nothing
white
sky
if
o


The dot must be a bird, or a falling rock.

# STUDY FOR *THE COLOR OF DUSK*

now it's the wind that throws itself on light
retreating in a line of machination

these fluid reefs, these apostolic chambers
a pageless elegy for dancing

if I could play with this while walking —
*no time, no time,* the rabbit says

his passage dense with green determination
I cross that bridge and come to it (comfort it)

slender corridors of craven men
their eyes a dream

blue, an expiation

# MATTER OF TIME, 10

she is not jesting
she is not asleep

here's the news:
Jiminy Cricket, friend,

it's time!
when the line falters

an idea sprouts
illustrating gnomon

must she have reason?
the center gravitates

to the sigh of signs
she can't hear

she can't see
beads of matter

on an axial neck
tra la la

oh, in the morning air
the landscape percolates

*I* and the rest follows
dragging its prey

which deity is this?
she came not into this show

to defend herself
she was called

there were caverns
she heated the pool

forever, she said
meaning nearly a year

of trying
the time before the time

when smoke rose
when wood fires burned

and games
adored her

less

# IN THE MUSEUM

We keel left. Verticals
protruding from the green
underbelly.

This works. This unreels.

The process undulates.

Only when the lights go out,
only when we huddle
in the semi-erotic darkness
does the vein hit.

Pergamon. The frieze.
Marbled heads captured
in their looming white.

Situated here, inside
themselves. Degas' horse,
the Russian bride.

Something's pushed against us —

We re-make God.

Sentence us, Lord.
Tell us the next
thousand years.

And then the next.

Lavender body, tree
pouring from its root.

Can this be memory?

# PRELUDE TO SILENCE

*To be in the book. To figure in the book of questions,*
*to be part of it. To be responsible for a word or a sentence,*
*a stanza or chapter.*

—EDMOND JABÈS

Word.

Page.

This object, objectified.

God in the book. God's word emulating silence. If we are suppressed. If this truth, too, explodes: invent phrases.

*Who if I cried? Who if I sang? Running my face through her hair —*

Suppositions, phrasings, in-breath, pause. Refrain, refrain. Where is it lodged, this God of yours?

Thus spoke Moses to the flock. The tablets hurled. Subject/object vying. Each half cracked. Wherein dwells the holy. Wherein dwells

I am not happy with the page. *I will evoke the book and provoke the questions.*

What word desires me?

Courage, courage. We are not dreaming. We are not yet dreaming. We are not yet

What word prepares the self for death?